G000135953

Magnificent
MINNIE
Hero

Magnificent MINNIE Hero

CLAIRE BARKER

MAXINE LEE-MACKIE

Collins

CONTENTS

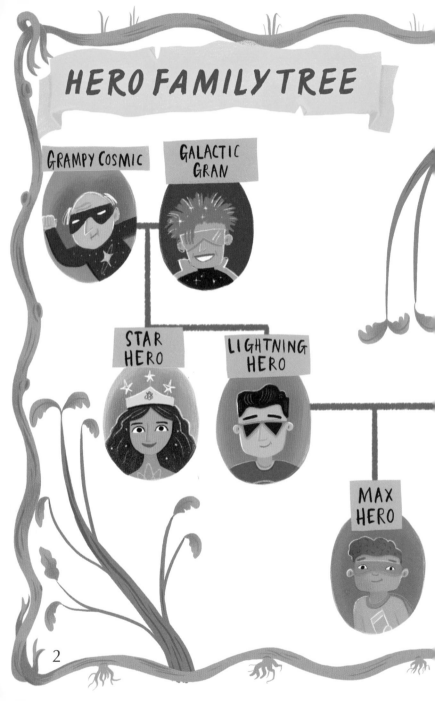

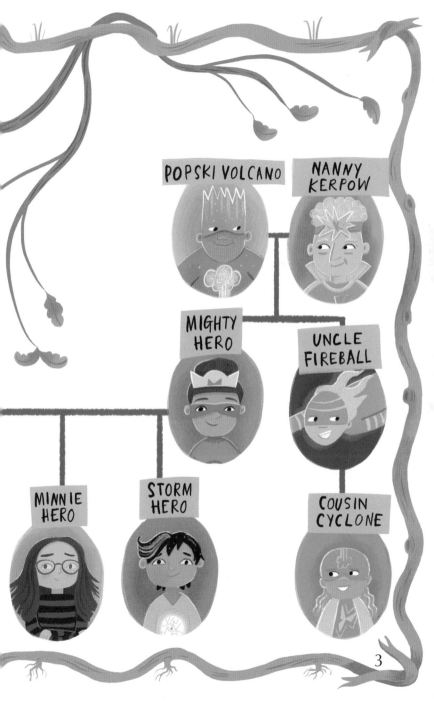

POPSKI VOLCANO

NANNY KERPOW

MIGHTY HERO

UNCLE FIREBALL

MINNIE HERO

STORM HERO

COUSIN CYCLONE

3

CHAPTER 1

Officially Minnie was a Hero, because it was her last name, but that was as far as it went. She wasn't super-fast like her dad, or super-strong like her mum. She wasn't super-loud like her big brother, or super-scary like her big sister.

Minnie Hero was small and quiet and ordinary. She wasn't interested in evil antiheroes or loud explosions. She refused to wear a costume because they were itchy and the superhero masks made her glasses slip.

"Do you think there's something wrong with her?" whispered Mrs Hero, looking out of the window at Minnie counting snails. "By her age, I was carrying the bus to school."

"It's just a matter of time," said Mr Hero. "You'll see." He leapt up from the table and began his thousand laps around the kitchen. "Soon it will be Minnie's birthday. I bet her superpowers will start then."

Mrs Hero sighed. "I hope so. It's just that sometimes – " She lowered her voice even further. "I worry she might be ... *normal*."

Mr Hero skidded to a halt, carving a deep groove in the floorboards. "Don't EVER say that. Everyone in our family has been a superhero; from Uncle Fireball and Cousin Cyclone to Grampy Cosmic and Galactic Gran. Minnie is no different."

But Minnie *was* different. Every day, while the rest of the family were busy practising their super-skills, Minnie slipped silently out of the gates of the mega-fortress. She cycled through the grey concrete city, down to the scrubby patch of green that was her local park.

Here she spent hours lying in the grass, watching the minibeasts and plants. Minnie couldn't see far without her glasses, but she could see close-up things really well. She loved studying tiny details, such as the rainbow flash of a fly's wing or the soft fur on the back of a bee. She kept a notebook full of drawings and notes, all about her bug discoveries. She was very proud of it.

But when she showed it to her big brother Max, he wasn't impressed. "FLIES AND WORMS DON'T MATTER, MINNIE," he boomed. "SUPERHEROES ARE LARGER THAN LIFE BECAUSE BIG PROBLEMS CALL FOR BIG SOLUTIONS."

"Yes," said her big sister, Storm, smashing a boulder into dust. "We're interested in epic disasters, not tiny insects. You're a Hero, Minnie, and it's about time you started acting like one."

Minnie pushed her glasses back up her nose
with a sigh. How could she tell them the truth,
that she was perfectly happy just as she was?
Yes, superheroes were impressive, but they never
drew pictures or went on walks or made cakes.
No one in the superhero community joined
a swimming club or played football. No one had
any sort of hobby.

Whenever other superhero families came over, everyone spent the whole time showing off and smashing things.

The truth was they were a bit dull. Not one of them had anything to say about the battles of stag beetles, or the amazing life cycle of dragonflies. Minnie saw the world differently to them. She noticed the little things, and through her eyes, their life didn't look very super at all.

Tomorrow was Minnie's tenth birthday and the traditional deadline for any super-talents to appear. Her older brother's powers had appeared on his first birthday, when he had said MUMMY and the sonic boom had knocked out the cat. Her sister's powers appeared on her third birthday, when the heat of her rage melted her tricycle. Minnie, however, had stayed normal for nearly *ten whole years*.

That night, she was so worried that she barely slept. *What if I wake up and suddenly want to explode something?* she thought. *Or I stop caring about nature and instead spend all my time worrying about how big my biceps are?*

Minnie's full name was Mindblower, and sometimes her mum called her that, because she thought it might help Minnie develop superpowers. But Minnie asked her to stop. Mindblower was a silly name, and Minnie suited her much better.

She reached under her pillow, pulled out her notebook and hugged it close to her heart. Minnie wanted everything to stay the same. "*Please* don't let me turn into a superhero tomorrow," she wished. "That would be the best birthday gift of all."

INSECT NOTES

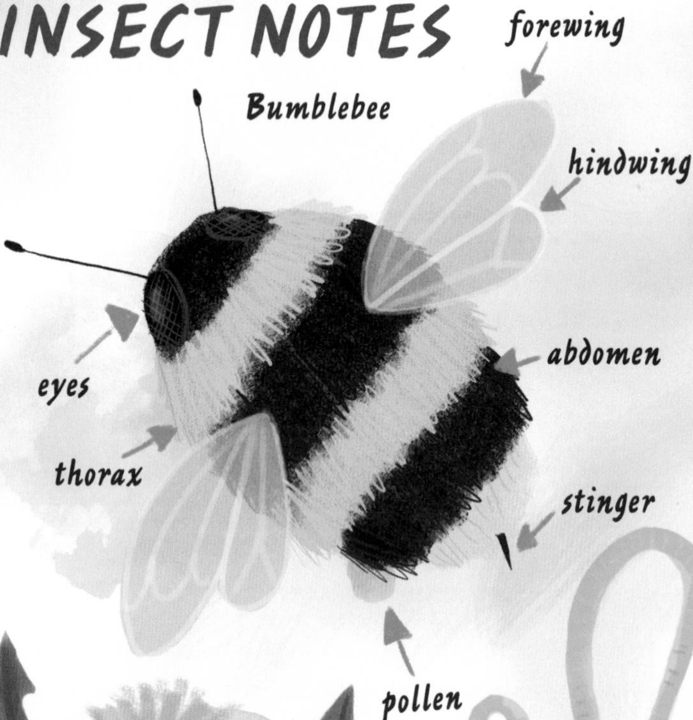

forewing

Bumblebee

hindwing

eyes

abdomen

thorax

stinger

pollen

Dandelion: Lots of nectar and pollen.

A wonderful plant for insects

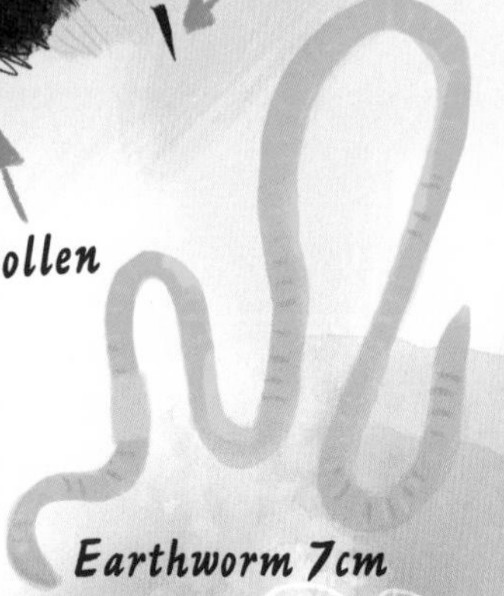

Earthworm 7cm
rescued from puddle

spider in the hedge

14

Ladybird

1 cm

Don't know what this is!
Must look up:

5 mm

Ivy flowers

I ♥ BUGS

Weather today

Shield bug 1.3 cm

Insects really seem to love ivy.

no rain

warm

bit of mud

Oops!

PARK POEM BY MINNIE HERO
Worms and soil below me
Moths and trees above
Park, you are my special place
This is what I love.

15

CHAPTER 2

The next morning, Minnie jumped out of bed and raced straight to the mirror. She nervously inspected herself for an extra super-something that might have appeared overnight. Were her teeth sparkly? Were her muscles bigger? No, she was still perfectly ordinary. She smiled at her reflection.

As Minnie shuffled downstairs in her pyjamas and bunny slippers, the loud singing began.

HAPPY BIRTHDAY TO YOU
YOU CAN BE SUPER TOO
SMASH BADDIES TO PIECES
ZAP! CRASH! BANG! WOO-HOO!

This was followed by a deafening round of applause that made the floorboards shake and pictures fall off the walls.

"*So . . .* how are you feeling, Minnie?" asked Dad, looking at her hopefully. "Anything different today?"

"Not yet, Dad." Minnie felt an unexpected twinge of sadness. As much as she wanted to be normal, she didn't like disappointing her family. They might be annoying, but she still loved them.

"Come on, Minnie, open your presents!" said Mum, holding the kitchen table one-handed above her head. On top was a tower of gifts, wrapped in paper and ribbons.

Minnie sat on the floor and opened them one by one. There was an instruction booklet called *How to Find the Super You*, a T-shirt that said KERPOW! and a packet of extra-strong vitamins. There was a silky cape, a step-by-step guide to dismantling bombs and a framed picture of the Hero family tree.

"Thank you, everyone," she said, smiling politely.

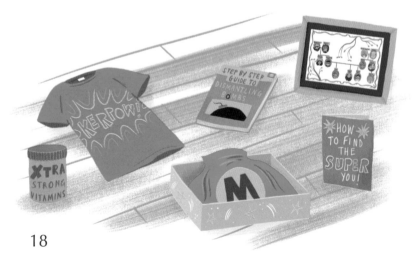

BUZZZZZ!

Alarmed, the family sprang to attention.
They leapt into power-stances, hands on hips,
legs astride. When they eventually realised it was
just the front doorbell, everyone calmed down.
(This sort of thing happened quite a lot.)
Dad zoomed downstairs and was back in a flash,
holding a small rectangular parcel.

"It's for you," he said, handing it to Minnie.
On the front, in tiny writing, it said:

For Miss Minnie Hero,
on her special day.

The Heroes gathered around. "Who can it be from?" asked Mum. "All of the family's gifts have been opened."

Minnie tore off the brown paper, revealing a cardboard box. She carefully lifted the lid. Inside, wrapped in tissue paper, lay an antique magnifying glass.

"Is that all?" said Storm, aghast. "What a rubbish gift. Hope they don't send *me* any birthday presents, whoever they are!"

Minnie picked the magnifying glass up and admired the smooth brass handle in her palm. She closed one eye and squinted through the curved glass with the other. It was the perfect present for a young naturalist. Having a proper magnifying glass was going to take her notebook to a whole new level. She couldn't wait to get down to the park to try it out.

After a quick breakfast of cereal, Minnie slipped away unnoticed. She put her notebook in her backpack and her magnifying glass in her pocket. She pedalled her bike out of the gates and zoomed down the hill like the wind. This was exactly how she wanted to spend her tenth birthday.

Once she reached the park, Minnie stopped every now and then to inspect things with her new present. It was amazing. Normally, she could see things well if she put her face very close, but with the magnifying glass she could see so much more. All at once, she could look into the eyes of flies and at the hairs on leaves. A bee looked up and waved his leg at her.

Minnie sat down, took out her notebook and began to make little sketches, resting the magnifying glass carefully on the grass.

The day was beautiful. Shafts of sunlight made everything shimmer, from the silvery threads of cobwebs to the muddy water in the old birdbath. The magnifying glass gleamed brightly. To her surprise, Minnie noticed that there were words engraved into the rim.

She picked it up and squinted closely, because the words were very, very small. Minnie read them out loud to herself:

"Magnificent .... Minnie ... ON"

Magnificent? What did that mean? Minnie's eyes widened as she suddenly understood. "Oh no … this can't be happening!" She sprang to her feet and dropped the magnifying glass in horror. She could hardly breathe. "OH NO!"

Then everything went black.

CHAPTER 3

Minnie gradually opened her eyes, squinting in the sunlight. The world was very colourful and bright. What had just happened and where was she? Minnie stretched her arms out and pushed her fingers into a thick bed of fur. She was lying on a big rug. It was yellow and black, stripy and soft. It was warm, trembling and smelt sweetly familiar.

Soon it began vibrating so hard that Minnie's teeth began to clatter inside her head. The rug lifted into the air and the noise was deafening. Was she in some sort of helicopter? Minnie rolled onto her tummy and held on tight, her fists full of fur. Then she understood. Minnie wasn't in a helicopter or on a flying carpet. She was clinging to the back of a giant bumblebee!

Below, the park raced by, as they flew past the rusty swings and overflowing bins. The wind in her face was so strong she could barely breathe. With a jerk, the bee swerved sideways, and Minnie lost her grip. **ARGH!**

She plummeted downwards, falling head over heels and landing with a loud, cold splash.

Minnie bobbed up like a cork, spluttering.
Where am I now? she thought. *I don't remember
a lake in the park.* Minnie looked around, trying to
get her bearings. As she did, a huge black dinosaur
flapped out of the sky and landed on the shore, with
a snake in its beak.

Minnie tried to stay calm. "Wait a minute," she said, treading water and trying to make sense of her surroundings. "The park doesn't have a lake and dinosaurs are extinct. I think this must be the *birdbath*, which means … oh no! The creatures aren't giant. It's me! I've shrunk to the size of a ladybird! She splashed angrily at the water. "Stupid superhero powers! Stupid birthday present!"

The blackbird cocked its head at all
the squeaking and splashing. It swallowed
the worm in one great, big gulp. Minnie realised
that if she didn't shut up, she was likely to end up as
a snack too.

Silently, she dived down under the muddy
water and swam to the far edge of the birdbath.
Beneath her, moss swirled around her legs like
seaweed, and strange small creatures swam
alongside her. Is this what the world looked
like when you were an insect? She didn't like it.
Minnie was scared and wanted to go home.

Dripping wet, she clambered down the ivy on the side of the birdbath. It was all going quite well, until a gust of wind scooped her up and dumped her – PLOP – into a nearby hedge. Minnie tumbled down through the branches *ouch-ouch-ouch* until she landed in a soft, springy hammock. *At least I'm lucky with soft landings* she thought, trying to look on the bright side.

But when Minnie went to sit up, she found she couldn't. Worse, the more she wriggled, the more her body stuck to the hammock's silvery threads.

Slowly, a huge, hairy beast emerged from behind a distant leaf. Its eight eyes were glittering. Minnie had admired the garden cross spider many times, but from this angle it looked very different. *Don't move, Minnie,* she thought, *but think fast!*

Fighting her rising terror, she tried to be logical. She needed to work backwards and undo everything. How had she shrunk in the first place? Of course! The inscription on the magnifying glass: *Magnificent Minnie ON.* So, what if she said "off", instead? That seemed stupidly simple, but really, a lot of superhero stuff was.

In a very quiet voice, so as not to alert the spider, she whispered:

"Magnificent Minnie OFF."

Nothing happened. In a slightly louder voice, she said it again. Nothing happened again.

But this time the spider heard her and sprang into the web. It started to race towards her, fangs clacking and hairy legs motoring. Terrified, Minnie yelled as loud as she could:

"MAGNIFICENT MINNIE *OFF*!"

When she awoke, she was back to full size, and lying next to the hedge, only a few steps away from where she had started that morning. The bees hummed and the water in the birdbath twinkled. A blackbird sang in the tree. The magnifying glass sat innocently beside her.

Minnie lay panting on the grass, her pulse racing. This was her worst birthday *ever*.

CHAPTER 4

At breakfast the next morning, Mr Hero wiped away a tear and patted Minnie's hand. "We want you to know that we are still proud of you."

"Having a superpower isn't that important," trilled Mrs Hero, unconvincingly. "We're just pleased that you have a hobby. Creepy-crawlies, isn't it? In that place down the road? Lots of weeds?"

"SHE LOVES BUGS!" yelled Max, shovelling power yoghurt into his mouth.

"Yuck!" said her sister, kicking the door off its hinges. "Disgusting."

Minnie never thought she would agree with her family, but yesterday's horror show had made her look at things differently. Maybe insects *were* disgusting. It had been so frightening that it had made her put her notebook away.

Back up in her room, she held the magnifying glass in her hand. If she *had* to have a superpower, why couldn't it be something simple, like being able to make fog or bad smells? This thing was dangerous. She couldn't risk something so scary happening again.

Minnie decided there was only one thing for it. She crossed over to her wardrobe and slammed the door against the magnifying glass. The lens shattered and dozens of shards spilt all over the floor.

Minnie swept them up and put them in the bin, feeling a huge sense of relief. But when she looked in the bin a minute later, the magnifying glass was there, whole again.

Determined to get rid of it, she opened her window and hurled it outside, watching it smash on the concrete below. But when she turned around it was resting on her bed, gleaming and as good as new. "Stupid super-objects," she muttered darkly. Clearly, she was just going to have to get used to the magnifying glass, as it wasn't going anywhere.

Minnie inspected the box it came in, searching for clues. Who had sent it? She took the box apart and, as she did, a small note fluttered out.

Metamorphosis
Love from
Tiny

Who? Minnie picked up the framed picture of the family tree that she had received for her birthday. There were lots of superheroes on it but no mention of anyone called Tiny.

Minnie leant out of her window again. "Dad!" she shouted, "Who's Tiny?"

Mr Hero was speeding around the fortress in a blur. "Can't stop now, Minnie, I'm about to break my personal record!"

Minnie sat back on her bed and looked at the message again. *Metamorphosis.* She knew what it meant, of course, every insect fan did. Metamorphosis was when a creature transformed itself, for example, when a caterpillar turned into a butterfly.

In the cosy gloom of her bedroom, Minnie looked at her reflection in the mirror. A small, timid-looking girl stared back at her. Was *she* in a cocoon? Was that what the message meant? That the time had come for her to spread her wings? Ten *was* quite big, after all.

Minnie frowned thoughtfully. Maybe she needed to look at it from a different viewpoint. Perhaps yesterday's shrinking had been so scary because she hadn't known what she was doing.

She thought about the first time that she rode her bike. She had wobbled, fallen off and grazed her knees. But with practice, she got much better and now cycling was one of her best things to do. It was close to flying.

Minnie held the magnifying glass in her hand. Now that she'd figured out how it worked, maybe she didn't need to be *scared*. Maybe she just needed to be *careful*. Bugs weren't horrible, they were incredible. Being able to shrink down to the size of a ladybird was pretty amazing. She couldn't deny that making notes from a bug's eye view would be brilliant.

Minnie started to cheer up. Maybe this would turn out to be the perfect superpower for her, after all.

That morning, Minnie cycled back to the park, found a quiet corner and took out the magnifying glass. She bent down and, with the tips of her fingers, she held on tight to the stem of a daisy. In her other hand, she held the magnifying glass. Minnie took a deep breath and said:

"Magnificent Minnie ON!"

CHAPTER 5

When Minnie opened her eyes, her arms were wrapped around the hairy trunk of the flower. Above her a wide canopy of white daisy petals fluttered in the breeze. It had worked!

"Hello! You're back. I really hoped you would be."

Minnie jumped. Who was that? She turned to see a brown moth gazing at her. A talking moth! Minnie didn't know what to say. Luckily, the moth was chatty enough for the two of them.

"I saw you yesterday, stuck in the spider's web," continued the moth. I thought you were about to be his dinner! It was very scary." The moth fluttered towards her, peering at her with big, brown eyes. "You're quite unique. Are you rare?"

"I'm … I'm a human. My name's Minnie."

"A hew-man," repeated the moth. "I've not heard of those. My name's Barbara. I live in the hedge. There's only one of me left here, so I'm always looking for new friends." She inspected Minnie closely. "I really like your big, shiny eyes, you must be able to see very well with those. They're detachable too! How amazing."

"I suppose they *are* amazing, when you put it like that," smiled Minnie, straightening her glasses.

"You don't have wings though, do you? Not to worry, not everyone does. I'll take you on a ride around the park, if you like. Am I talking too much? I'm not supposed to be awake in the daytime, but my thoughts are extra busy at this time of year."

Minnie laughed. Barbara was very nice. "Yes, please. Thank you very much."

As she rose into the sky, Minnie knew straightaway that this was going to be much better than the bee ride. Minnie admired Barbara's wings: a tawny tapestry seemingly made of dust and silk. Minnie tried hard to remember the pattern so she could draw it later.

Barbara's wings moved silently through the air. Minnie could hear a *tramp tramp tramp* below them quite clearly. "What's that noise?" she asked curiously.

"That's the ants on their daily march. They are extremely fit."

Suddenly, a huge green monster appeared mid-air, right next to Minnie's face. But before she had a chance to scream, it disappeared again!

"Morning, grasshopper," called Barbara.

"Good morning, Barbara."

"He's an amazing singer *and* athlete,"
said Barbara. "Actually, at first, I thought you must
be a grasshopper too. You know, the way you
suddenly appear and disappear. Oh, look down
there, Minnie, it's the Woodlouse family. Give them
a wave."

Lots of woodlice were standing on a log, waving
their little legs and chorusing, "Hello, Barbara!"

"Hello, everyone. You're all invited to a party
at my house to welcome our new friend, Minnie.
Tell all the beetles and the hoverflies. See you over at
The Hedge."

Very soon, Minnie found herself in the middle of a tiny tea party.

The woodlice shared their dead leaves with the beetles and the hoverflies shared their pollen. Barbara sipped a twinkling drop of nectar from a yellow flower.

"Everyone! I've gathered you all here to meet our new friend, Minnie," said Barbara, "but also to share important news. As you know, I've been very busy lately." Barbara fluttered over to a nearby section of the hedge and settled on a leaf. It was covered in tiny eggs. "I am happy to announce that soon there will be lots of baby Barbaras!"

Everyone cheered, including Minnie. They danced and ate, sang songs and listened to the whispers of the trees.

The celebrations went on and on until Barbara said she couldn't stay awake a moment longer.

"Come back soon, Minnie," she yawned, stretching her wings. "I'll introduce you to the centipedes next time. They love having their feet tickled. The giggling is hilarious!"

"I've had the best time ever," said Minnie, "I'll see you tomorrow."

Barbara fluttered back into the hedge. Minnie said the magic words, loud and clear, and sprang back to her normal size.

As she cycled back home, she was so glad that she hadn't given up on the magnifying glass. Bugs were glorious!

Brimming with happiness, Minnie pushed open the heavy front door of the fortress. She noticed the local newspaper lying on the hall table. The headline read:

DAILY TRUMPET

PARK TO BE DEMOLISHED TO MAKE WAY FOR COUNCIL CAR PARK

WORK TO BEGIN TODAY

CHAPTER 6

"Don't cry, Minnie," said Mr Hero, putting his arm around her.

"We'll find you another park," said Mrs Hero.

"Yes," said Mr Hero. "There's a great one only 3,000 kilometres from here. I'll take you."

"NO!" sobbed Minnie. "I don't want to go to another park. I love MY park. My friends live there."

Storm kindly offered to smash the diggers to pieces.

"GREAT IDEA!" boomed Max.

"Yes!" said Mrs Hero. "We shall destroy their machines with speed and strength! Tell us the enemy's name!"

"It's the council," sniffed Minnie.

Mr Hero checked the List of Official Antiheroes. "The council's not in here."

Mrs Hero shrugged. "Sorry. We aren't allowed to fight baddies that aren't on the list. There's a special form."

Minnie couldn't believe her ears. "Are you saying that all of your superpowers are useless in the face of *paperwork*?"

"Calm down. It's not the end of the world," said Storm. "It's only some bugs and weeds."

"It is NOT just bugs and weeds, it's an *entire ecosystem*!" shouted Minnie. "Insects are key to our survival! Don't you know that? If you really want to save the world, you should start by reading!"

The rest of the Hero family looked shocked. Was this true?

Minnie ran upstairs to her bedroom and slammed the door. She had to save the park, but how?

Maybe, if she explained to the council, they would listen. But Barbara was just a little brown moth. What was so special about that? Utterly miserable, Minnie went straight to her Bug Guide.
Flicking through the pages, her eye was caught by a familiar image. Minnie gasped. "I'd know that wing pattern anywhere – it's Barbara!"

As she read the text next to the picture, her eyes widened and a smile spread across her face. The information was right under her nose.

Her bedroom door blasted open, revealing the Heroes, posed and ready for action.

"You were right, Minnie," said Mum. "Our world is DOOMED without insects! Nature is in crisis! We just read about it on the internet."

Minnie held up the Bug Guide, her eyes bright. "It turns out that research is a superpower too. Let's go!"

Mr Hero whizzed them all to the park at lightning speed. Within seconds, the whole family was blocking the diggers.

"HALT!" bellowed Max. "ALL MUST LISTEN TO MY LITTLE SISTER!"

A newspaper reporter stepped out of the crowd and began to take notes.

Standing on Mrs Hero's head, Minnie straightened her glasses, held up her book and began.

"This park is home to the *extremely rare* barberry carpet moth. It is an endangered species and is fully protected by law. You're not allowed to disturb this important habitat. What you are doing is illegal. Take one step further and I shall be forced to call the police."

A council official stepped forward. "Get out of our way, little girl."

"NO!" Minnie's voice was so loud it surprised even Max. "I'll show you! Follow me."

Minnie marched over to the hedge. "Look at these yellow flowers. This is a barberry bush and the barberry carpet moth depends on its nectar and leaves."

The council official smirked. "So what? Where's the moth? Because I can't see it."

Minnie leant into the hedge and hissed, "Psst. Barbara, please wake up. It's me, Minnie. *BARBARA!*"

The council officer tutted. "Start the digger."

"NO!" said Minnie in despair. What about Barbara's babies? "Her eggs! You can't!"

The digger roared into life, gnashing its teeth, like a terrible, mechanical lion.

Then, at the very last moment, a little brown moth fluttered sleepily out of the hedge. She landed right on the tip of Minnie's nose.

"Phew," said Minnie.

There was a FLASH as a reporter took a photo, and then a CRASH as Storm crushed the digger.

"What I don't understand," said Mrs Hero,
"is how Minnie was able to summon that little moth.
It's not as if she has any superpowers."

"You know, I think I remember an elderly relative who could do that," said Mr Hero, leafing through his new wildlife annual. "All sorts of bugs followed her about. She didn't have superpowers, though. Dear old Tiny."

Listening from the next room, Minnie smiled. She polished her glasses and put them back on her nose. Everything was much clearer now.

She picked up her trusty magnifying glass and headed for the door.

"If anyone needs me, I'll be at the park," called Minnie, "saving the world!"

TWO DIARIES

Dear Diary,

I still haven't told my family about my superpowers. If they think I can shrink, I might have to do normal superhero stuff, but my destiny is to protect bugs. I wonder if Tiny felt the same?

Minnie

Dear Diary,

Minnie is in all the newspapers.
How wonderful! I'm so glad
the magnifying glass is perfect for her,
just as it was for me. It seems she has
kept her superpowers secret, just as
I did. Very wise. The bugs are safe in
her hands.

Tiny Hero

MINNIE BEASTS GALORE!

"BARBARA'S PARADISE" CELEBRATES FIRST ANNIVERSARY

Wildlife experts are amazed by Minnie Hero's talent for finding rare plants and animals! In the past year, Minnie has been busy on the new wildlife reserve, Barbara's Paradise. She has discovered four kinds of butterfly, six new slime moulds and a very rare flower. Environmental groups all around the world have asked for Minnie's help.

But local hero Minnie has no plans to go anywhere just yet. With the help of her wildlife-mad family, she plans to do even more for the local environment. They will be planting more trees and wildflowers, digging ponds and building bug hotels.

"Wherever you live, being a nature hero begins with your local area," said Minnie, with a big smile. "Saving the world starts with small steps!"

MINNIE'S BUG GUIDE

BARBERRY CARPET MOTH — *RARE*

when active: at night

size: wingspan around 3cm

depends on: barberry leaves

lives: in hedgerows

GARDEN CROSS SPIDER – COMMON

when active: mainly at night

size: 5mm to 2cm

eats: butterflies, wasps and flies

lives: large round webs in gardens and woods

INCREDIBLE INSECTS!

Did you know? ...

Butterflies taste
with their feet.

sunflower

Honeybees vibrate to
keep warm in winter.

Hoverflies might look like
bees, but they don't sting.

foxglove

Spider silk is the strongest natural fibre in the world!

There are more than **2,500** kinds of moth in the UK.

barberry bush

thistle

Some ants explode when they are attacked!

About the author

A bit about me …

I live in the countryside with my family and an assortment of (quite naughty) animals. I write stories in a little hut on wheels, at the end of a wild garden.

Claire Barker

How did you get into writing?

I was doing an illustration course at a local college. One of the projects was to write to an agent, so I painted some fairy-tale characters and put them in an envelope. I was about to put them in the postbox when, at the last minute, I decided to include some funny letters. To my astonishment, the agent wrote back straight away, said they liked the letters best of all and had I thought of being a writer? Since then I've written 11 books.

What is it like for you to write?

Sometimes it's hard, because my brain is always trying to start something brand new, which can make it difficult to concentrate on the task in hand. But when I am deep in a story the words come fast and loud, like the sound of galloping horses. It's thrilling.

What book do you remember loving when you were young?

I loved *The Beano* annuals and had a huge pile on the end of my bed. I also had a special book of bedtime stories based on Shakespeare's plays.

Why did you want to write this book?

There have been a lot of superhero stories lately. But, in light of global warming, what does "saving the world" mean in the 21st century? Unfortunately, I suspect that glamorous costumes and dramatic explosions aren't going to get us very far. So I wanted to write about a different sort of superhero; one that children could identify with, one that would use their powers wisely.

Do you identify with any of the characters in the story? If so, who, and why?

Like Minnie, I've worn glasses all my life. It occurred to me that superheroes never seem to be short-sighted and I wondered why not? Superman only pretends to need glasses when he's trying to appear normal. I thought this was silly, so made sure Minnie wore hers all the time and that the insects thought they were terrific.

What do you hope readers will get out of the book?

I hope they will be inspired to learn the names of a few of the plants and insects that are in their local area. This might seem like a small thing, but who knows where it will lead? Barbara shows us that even a little brown moth can turn out to be something quite extraordinary. Through caring about the plants and creatures around them, children really can truly help to save the world.

If you could have a superpower, what would it be?

I would send a trance around the world to make grown-ups care less about money and more about living things.

71

About the illustrator

What made you want to be an illustrator?

I've always loved the colours and tools involved with drawing, especially pencils and drawing pads. I love the way they look, and smell, and feel. I knew from a young age that I wanted to draw and paint as much as possible.

Maxine Lee-Mackie

How did you get into illustration?

When I left school, I did some research and spoke to illustrators who I looked up to. They gave me some advice and helped me to improve my skills. I experimented with different methods until I felt confident enough to approach clients.

What did you like best about illustrating this book?

Like Minnie, I love insects and nature, so I was really excited about spending time researching and drawing bugs and flowers. I especially loved illustrating Barbara.

What was the most difficult thing about illustrating this book?

Drawing the spiders. I'm not their biggest fan, but I'm working on it! I'd rather see one outside than in my house.

Is there anything in this book that relates to your own experiences?

I don't always feel like I fit in with everyone else, and I love to help others who don't have a voice – just like Minnie.

How do you bring a character to life in an illustration?

I think about their interests, age, culture and lifestyle. All of those things help me to form a picture in my mind of what they might wear, how they might style their hair, and even the kind of bag they might carry.

What superpower would you like to have?

I think Minnie's superpower is pretty cool. At the moment, I have to use a macro lens to get really close to insects to photograph them so I can see them close up. Being able to see them like that with my own eyes would be amazing. Not sure I'd want to be that close to a spider that was bigger than me though!

Did any particular books or films inspire you when you were thinking about what the characters should look like?

Yes, they did! I used to love comics when I was small, especially Minnie the Minx from *The Beano*, who always wore a black-and-red striped top. That's as far as the inspiration goes though, because Minnie the Minx is very different to Minnie Hero.

Did you like reading superhero comics and stories when you were a child?

I did! The ones I liked best were Spiderman, Wonder Woman and Bananaman.

Book chat

Apart from Minnie, who was your favourite character, and why?

What do you think about the way that Minnie's family treated her in this story?

Is there a villain in this story? Explain your answer.

Does the book remind you of any other books you've read? How?

Would you like to read another book that follows on from this one? If so, what might be in it?

If you could talk to one character from the book, who would you pick? What would you say to them?

Do any characters in the book remind you of someone you know in real life? If so, how?

If you could ask the author one question, what would it be?

Do you think Minnie changed between the start of the story and the end? If so, how?

Book challenge:

Look outside, see how many plants and animals you can spot!

Published by Collins
An imprint of HarperCollins*Publishers*

The News Building
1 London Bridge Street
London SE1 9GF
UK

Macken House
39/40 Mayor Street Upper
Dublin 1
D01 C9W8
Ireland

Text © Claire Barker 2023
Design and illustrations © HarperCollins*Publishers*
Limited 2023

10 9 8 7 6 5 4

ISBN 978-0-00-862474-3

All rights reserved. No part of this publication
may be reproduced, stored in a retrieval system, or
transmitted in any form by any means, electronic,
mechanical, photocopying, recording or otherwise,
without the prior written permission of the Publisher
or a licence permitting restricted copying in
the United Kingdom issued by the Copyright
Licensing Agency Ltd, 5th Floor, Shackleton House,
4 Battle Bridge Lane, London SE1 2HX.

British Library Cataloguing-in-Publication Data
A catalogue record for this publication is available
from the British Library.

Download the teaching notes and
word cards to accompany this book at:
http://littlewandle.org.uk/signupfluency/

Get the latest Collins Big Cat news at
collins.co.uk/collinsbigcat

Author: Claire Barker
Illustrator: Maxine Lee-Mackie (The Bright Agency)
Publisher: Lizzie Catford
Product manager: Caroline Green
Series editor: Charlotte Raby
Development editor: Catherine Baker
Commissioning editor: Suzannah Ditchburn
Project manager: Emily Hooton
Content editor: Daniela Mora Chavarría
Copyeditor: Sally Byford
Phonics reviewer: Rachel Russ
Proofreader: Gaynor Spry
Cover designer: Sarah Finan
Typesetter: 2Hoots Publishing Services Ltd
Production controller: Katharine Willard

Collins would like to thank the teachers and
children at the following schools who took part in
the trialling of Big Cat for Little Wandle Fluency:
Burley And Woodhead Church of England Primary
School; Chesterton Primary School; Lady Margaret
Primary School; Little Sutton Primary School;
Parsloes Primary School.

Printed and bound in the UK by Page Bros Group Ltd

MIX
Paper | Supporting
responsible forestry
FSC
www.fsc.org
FSC™ C007454

This book contains FSC™ certified paper and other controlled
sources to ensure responsible forest management.

For more information visit: www.harpercollins.co.uk/green